ISBN: 9781990700521

Printed in the U.S.A.

Visit us on the web at: www.lifetopaper.com

First Edition: 2024

Illustrated by: Julie Tait

Life to Paper Publishing
Miami | Toronto

LIFE TO PAPER
PUBLISHING

Georange Horange's Storange

Written by Ryan Tait
Illustrations by Julie Tait

Dedicated to the late "Toy Doctor", Dale Zimmerman
and all the children of Sunny View Public School.

Georange Horange was an organized orange
who always had a smile on his face.

When playing at home, Georange always worked hard
to store his toys in their place.

Georange was a student at Sunny View School
for children with varying abilities.

The children at Sunny View
learned all that they could,
with assistance to complete
their activities.

Georange loved his school,
it had wonders abound.

It was even equipped with
an indoor playground.

It had koi fish, plants
and spaces to play
with really cool toys that
were used everyday.

These toys were not found at any other schools.
They were built and invented with hammers
and tools.

The lady who built them was Toy Doctor Dale.
Just sit back and read and I'll tell you a tale.

At recess she'd watch all the children have fun,
then go to her shop to build toys not yet done.

Toy Doctor Dale always built what kids need,
to have fun at recess and also succeed.

She built tickling toys, light up toys, toys that looked fizzy,
spinning toys, toys that flew and toys that made you dizzy.

Georange would spend his recess
helping children play around.

By reaching for the items that
they'd dropped onto the ground.

One day in the Adventure Centre, Georange was looking sad.
"Nothing rhymes with orange!" he'd learned,
which made him ill a tad.

When Toy Doctor Dale
saw his sad crying face,
she found a solution,
she had just the place.

After a few days working hard in her shop,
she'd built something new to make
his sad feelings stop.

What she built was a Storange, it opened up in six slices.
Five of which contained sensory devices.

First was the sight slice with bulbs of light.
Children pushed buttons to make colours shine bright.

Second was the smell slice, with scents that perked your nose.

One button smelled like coffee and another, stinky toes.

Third was the touch slice with toys
that felt icky.

Children touched textures which
before was very tricky.

Fourth was the hearing slice,
with speakers playing sounds.

Children pushed on buttons to hear
crickets, frogs or clowns.

Fifth was the taste slice, with a
super juice machine.

Children mixed up flavours that were
healthy, cold and green.

Sixth was the storage slice where toys were cleaned
and stored.

It's how the Storange got its name, and it started with a cord.

Georange was so excited to see the new
Storange invention, but getting it in the dictionary
would now be his intention.

If Storange was in the dictionary,
a real word it would be.

And orange would have a rhyming word,
which made Georange real happy.

Storange
Dictionary

So Toy Doctor Dale and Georange, sat and wrote a letter,
explaining to the dictionary, how the Storange made life better.

Sadly with the response mailed, they sat and read,
"Your mission failed.
Words in here are said by many.
Who says the word Storange?
Not any."

Dale told Georange, "Now don't get mad.
I have a plan to make you glad.
We must show the world your toy,
and show them all its fun and joy!"

It took a week and about a day,
to build enough to let all play.

The Storange would soon be well known,
once they'd all, been taught and shown.

They delivered one to every school.
They knew that kids would find it cool.

Any child who needed fun,
could play with this till they were done.

Once every school received their Storange,
Dale was pleased with little Georange.

The word was out and kids now knew,
so it was time for try number two.

A few weeks passed and time stood still.
Their nerves would last, they had strong wills.

Then when the letter showed up one day, Georange asked Dale,
"What does it say?"

They suddenly both felt really proud,
with a "Yes!" they both screamed loud.

The mission was done, Storange was in.
For Dale and Georange, it was a win!

The letter had an invitation, downtown near Union Station.
There a party and banner would say, Storange made it in today!

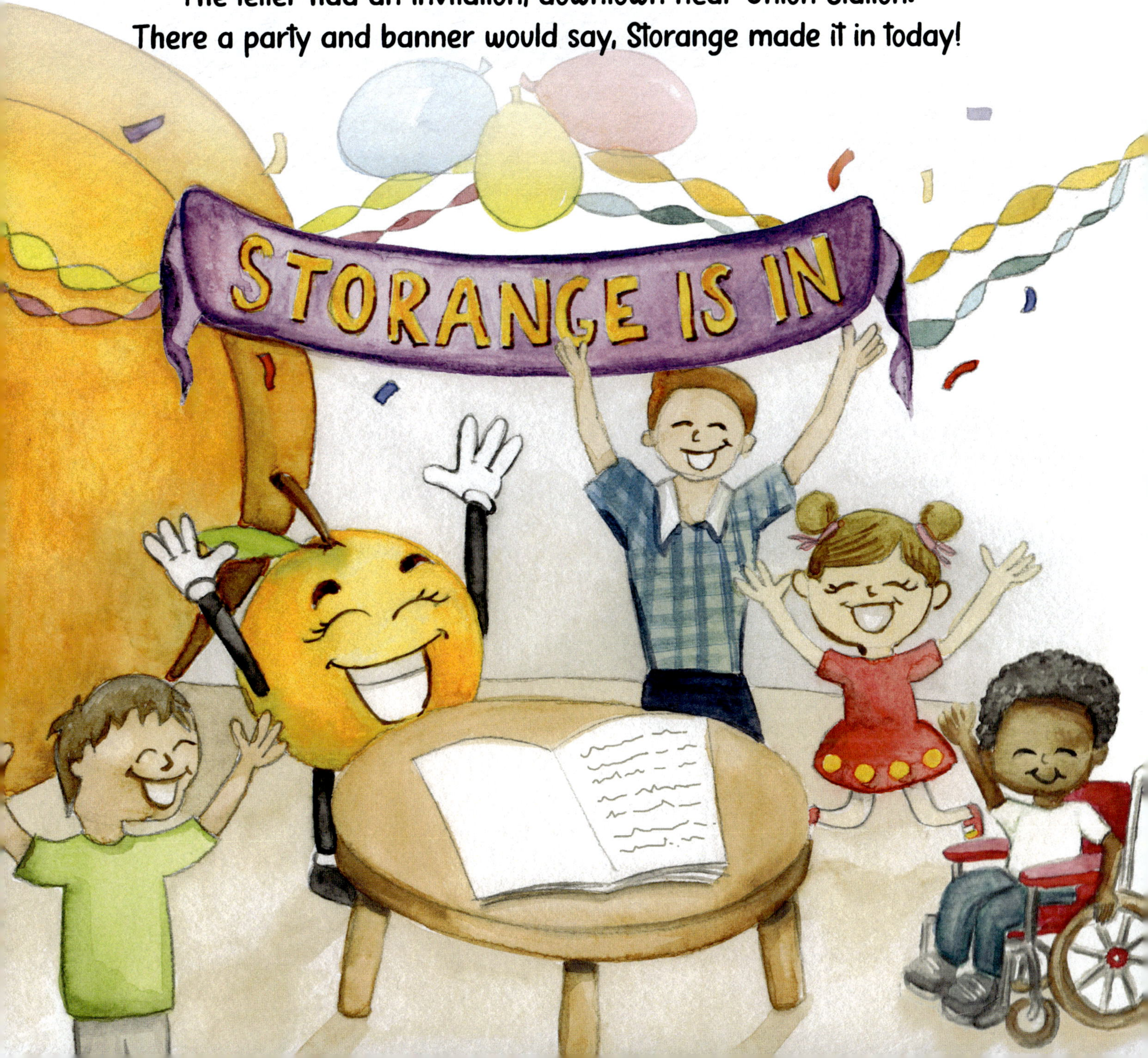

Toy Doctor Dale and Georange went on,
to prove impossible is two letters too long.

Ryan Tait is a Canadian author and Toy Doctor at the Sunny View School in Toronto, ON. If you'd like to support our program and help it grow, visit, Friends of Sunny View School Charity:
www.sunnyviewcharity.ca

Toydoctorer

Manufactured by Amazon.ca
Bolton, ON

39456973R00024